FIREWORKS
&
SPARROWS

4.10.94

Selected Poems

FIREWORKS
&
SPARROWS

by

S. S. CHARKIANAKIS

Translator
VRASIDAS KARALIS

Editor
SYBILLE SMITH

PRIMAVERA

SYDNEY

1994

This book may be ordered from the publisher, but try your bookshop first.

Primavera Press
PO Box 575
Leichhardt Sydney
Australia 2040
Call: 02 - 569 1452
Fax: 02 - 564 1548

Publisher—Paul Brennan

National Library of Australia Cataloguing-in-Publication entry:
Charkianakis, S. S. (Stylianos), 1935–
  Fireworks and Sparrows—Selected Poems

  Includes index.
  ISBN 1 875368 14 0 (limited ed.).
  ISBN 1 875368 15 9 (pbk.).

  1. Charkianakis, S. S. (Stylianos), 1935–
  Translations into English. I. Karalis, Vrasidas.
  II. Smith, Sybille. III. Title.

889.134

This project has been assisted by the Commonwealth Government through the Australia Council, its arts funding and advisory body

MANUFACTURED WHOLLY WITHIN AUSTRALIA

INSTEAD OF A PROLOGUE

Between earth and fire
    all your journeys;
your dreams green
your sadness nothing but yearning
for what is burnt to sprout again in your hands:
to accept a curse as a word of blessing.

1978

1

BALLAD OF THE NIGHT

Only during the night should you cry
in the late hours
        the hours of mist;
when the many who cry by day are sleeping
        only then should you cry.

Night knows secrecy, knows silence
and discretion is necessary
for those who seek
some joy from you.

Do not forget:
the crying of the brave
must be attended only by heaven
        and by silence,
the escort of all great moments.

Bonn
30.10.60

FOR THOSE WHO HATE THE LIGHT

For the great artist
there is no minor
or major work.
When a painter looks at his work
he sees his work;
when God wants you in life
He wants His work
and when He wants you in death
He wants His work.

Bonn
20.9.63

3

BELATED HOMECOMING

Is this the end?
Is this the beginning?
Unknown buildings and alien
vengeful winds chase away
      the silent tear.
There is no light left
to welcome you.

Thessalonica
10.9.67

4

EPITAPH

A skeleton of orphanhood
a sponge dry in the sea
with the saint's agony
a thief's experience.

Thessalonica
11.6.68

HYMN TO THE ANONYMOUS

O Thou beyond everything—
for how else can I sing Thee?
Gregory Nazianzus [1]

You are not Logic
because it has limits.
You are not Justice
because it knows conditions.
You are not Morality
because you transcend both act and mind.
You are not Freedom
because it can be restricted.
You are not Beauty
because it can be exhausted.
You are the Love which hasn't yet uttered
the final word.
The unpremeditated Love.
The ever-unanticipated Love.
Love you are, my only
unconditional condition.

Thessalonica
17. 6. 68

6

PASSUS MORTALIS

Thus an infant ever comes
into the world:
powerless, dumb, exhausted.
The horror that its eyes have seen
crossing the haunted bridge
from non-being to life,
paralysed its knees
took away its voice.

But soon it will forget
that alphabet
it whispered so persistently.
For a while it will ramble in the light
embracing shadows and ghosts
and then it will lose its voice forever
in death's unjustifiable silence.

Uppsala
9. 7. 68

7

KEEP LEFT

Untimely is mourning
      amid such vast melancholy;
you will be mocked by eucalypts
      by their multitude
      by their silence.

In such an ultimate desert
never complain of bereavement;
never speak of bitterness and tears
      in the antipodes of the earth.

People here have problems
      that are never resolved:
cyclones, sharks;
only the kangaroo
with its double stomach
reminds you of human measure.

Sydney
25.7.75

AUSTRALIA, 1975

God created this land
     for all people
poor mother of pain and refuge,
receiving the debris of the other world
and giving it back to the sun
     a glittering coin
in the dimensions of the Ocean and the Desert.

This land looks like the sea,
vast, challenging, untamed, virginal
with its bread rich and salty
with its embrace ambivalent
     in every kiss.

Darwin
24.10.75

9

REQUIEM FOR POETRY

If there is any light left
from our daily adventures,
it would become sighs in a climate of wonder
sorrows which became verses.

With such spells you struggle to postpone
              the death of beauty
by raising fireworks and sparrows
              against the most unjust conspiracy
of natural laws.

But how much light and feeling
              can words rescue?
Silently, they die too
leaving behind floating verses
              in the dominion of silence
flotsam of an undetected shipwreck,
still bearing witness
that the journey was made with faith.

Palm Beach
29.12.76

10

TRAFFIC

Every morning there begins between us
a day-long miracle of trust
despite all reservations and suspicions
despite all inconsistencies and contradictions.

Every morning we renew an oath
without exchanging a single word
ready for any possibility
in public vehicles, private or hired.

Every morning by going out of our homes
we dare an anonymous
an endless engagement
so that all the traffic around us
is transformed into our strongest emotion.

Brisbane
28.5.77

11

THE NOBLEST METAL

Cross yourself when you talk about the body.
Dimitris Maronitis [2]

Gold is not the noblest metal
neither platinum nor silver nor any of their like;
clay is the noblest mine,
clay from which the human body is made.
Our soul's weakness is the body
deep refuge and trust in identity
        sealed by blood.
And then say what you will
of hands, eyes, hair, tears ...

Ashfield, Sydney
1.8.79

12

ORIENTATION

Thou art careful and troubled about
many things: but one thing is needful:
Luke, 10, 41–2

All rivers which flow
whether in violence or indolence
have only one nostalgia:
the sea!

Ashfield, Sydney
7.3.80

THE MIRROR

Cover that mirror immediately
if you want some degree of inwardness
      inside your home, at least.
The door and the window are benevolent straits
securing our view, light, air;
but the mirror is a well of abysmal fraud
capriciously distorting dimensions
abandoning you, orphaned and wavering,
just when it feigns the warmest intimacy
the most faithful identity of things.
Any other surface is not simply a limit
      of orientation or stability;
it is also a landscape
of invisible cavities and undulations
      the Epiphany of a pulsing truth.
But the mirror does not embody
any landscape or limit: only the chaos of death
reflecting life mortified;
faithful to its indifferent, icy nature
      and moreover
to its detached and absolute brilliance ...

Adelaide
29.4.80

TO C. P. CAVAFY [3]

...where sin abounded, grace did much more abound.
Romans 5, 20

Your portrait I want to paint
Old Man, glorified out of your disgrace,
but not to denounce the voluptuousness
         of your omniscient eyes
behind your crumbling glasses.
I want rather to remind all barbarians,
apart from "remember Lord your servant for
         Thou art kind",
of how much bereavement must have purified you
in those dark labyrinths
of Alexandrian decadence
         which matured your soul.
I worked for years in silence
on this requiem-evocation
feeling the pulse of every concealment
in the few writings you left us
like the fine trail of the snail;
but overwhelmed by groping for the ineffable
your portrait I abandon for ever.
In its empty place I leave a wish:
"May your memory be eternal,
         blessed brother"
bitter bard of a fleeting eternity.

Ashfield, Sydney
12.1.81

15

ASSOCIATIONS

The dead man's beard and nails
    grow faster
like the branches of some strange
tropical tree on Magnetic Island
plunging to touch the earth
    and become roots
as though their own trunk was not enough to suckle.
But this urge to expand beyond limits
is not voracious;
the extremities, trembling in air,
sink to balance
    in the womb of life
longing for the ultimate homecoming.

East Bentleigh, Melbourne
22.2.81

16

ANTHROPOCENTRISM

Man is the measure of all things.
Protagoras [4]

The sacredness of the world is not inferred
from the narration of Genesis
since no one lived it
and pious thoughts are not compulsory.
The sacredness of the world is a consequence
of lived suffering unrecorded
by personal diaries or works of art
lacking as we do the appropriate means.
The sacredness of the world I pondered
seeing the thoughtful gaze of a passer-by
almost killed by a car
as he crossed the road absent-minded.

Ashfield, Sydney
9.1.83

17

INTENSIVE CARE

Poetry, brothers, is
neither song nor reflection.
Poetry is intensive care
over the bleeding Creation
and mostly recording
how life goes straight to death.

Ashfield, Sydney
25.1.83

THE HOUSE IN ASHFIELD

What a strange station that house is!
it belongs to many, it belongs to none.
A fearful phantom you can't catch
        a dream you enjoyed
        and know won't return.
It became haunted in its contradictions, that house.
Remote and majestic like a castle
yet close and defenceless
like a rose protruding from a fence.
Nevertheless despite all insecurity
it still secures a little sleep of peace
it shelters a few hours of comfort
        it is my home!

Dunk Island
14.2.84

TO MY MOTHER

In my study I keep always
a photograph of you five years ago
and I watch the wrinkles that settled on your face
and dry up now under the sun and air
like the face of the earth when a storm passes
and exposes everything to everyone
begging, it seems, a catholic absolution
in the absolute embarrassment of the finalised.
I glorify the light on the one hand which guides me
through the countless details of your face
and on the other I would like to switch it off
to stop it recording new ruins
        on the Earthly Jerusalem
the only one I have seen and worship.

Redfern, Sydney
24.7.85

MOTHER FORGIVE

Now that Crete has taken back its loan
deeply you sleep under your natal soil
without fear of your foot worsening
or the ominous signs of the blood tests.
You became serene already in your coffin
a secured infant in a cradle of worship
flowers with incense moistened your face
the first libation to your sudden metamorphosis!
But I who for fifty years struggled
with gods and demons under your shadow
how can I everafter endure the burning sun
unsheltered under the many winds, under the rain?
Mother, forgive this, my first feebleness.
I need time to get used to your absence
even though from the grave you will guide me
with your characteristic farewell:
"My child, I give you my best wish
and give me your benediction"!

Sydney–Brisbane
15.3.86

PAPER BOY

His whistle every morning
bears something indefinite like grief
whereas all it wants to state
is fresh newspapers for sale.
But reading the first pages you realise
that the grief is not indefinite
but very concrete.
The global financial crisis is in deadlock
juntas execute prisoners unpunished
nine-year-old kidnapped Samantha was not found
and earthquakes flattened Kalamata ...

Ashfield, Sydney
20.9.86

CONVERSATION

When we converse I am
neither the teacher nor the pupil;
only the enchanted I am who discovers
how fluid the limits of consciousness are.

Ashfield, Sydney
6.10.86

EVALUATION

Finally
all shapes are an attempt
to collaborate with the light.

Adelaide
22.10.86

THE FIRST RESURRECTION

The thrown stone of a peach
asks for the flesh you devoured
        five minutes ago
considering it spent.
Yet it ignores *faits accomplis*
it will sprout again in the soil
and complete its own odyssey
becoming a blooming tree
to perpetuate its vanished flesh.

Ashfield, Sydney
11.3.87

THE EVER-VIRGINITY OF LIFE

A torn shoe has its own story:
the love-affair with the road
the daily farewells
and the renewed meetings with the foot
but above all the distant memory
almost dissolved in the liquids of tanning
that one day this dyed hide
was a skin which suffered and felt cold.

Ashfield, Sydney
20.5.87

26

DEEPER COMMUNICATION

Collecting shells on the beach
you shake hands silently
   with the Invisible.

Great Keppel Island
15.11.87

EDIFICATION

Come, let us talk quietly
peacefully and without heat
as shadows converse on the wall.
Do you believe that with all our garrulity
we manage to say anything more
than the shadows manage to pronounce
                before sunset?
The more we simplify the code
of words and motions
the more we surpass
ashes and shades.

Ashfield, Sydney
10.12.87

28

DEFENCELESS INNOCENCE

*All manner of sin and blasphemy shall be
forgiven unto men: but the blasphemy against
the Holy Spirit shall not be forgiven ...*
Matthew 12, 31

The blank page is not simply a challenge
for experimentations of vanity.
It is the defenceless innocence
of the silent ones
which will judge till the end of time
any debauchery of the letter or the spirit
that *shall not be forgiven ...*

Sydney–Melbourne
31.10.87

MEMORIAL (B)

Why do you think I framed your picture?
Simply so that
your visage won't spread
    all over the wall
your visage won't expand
    in and out the house
so that my tearful eyes
    are unable to embrace you ...

Ashfield, Sydney
6.1.89

THE FACE OF THE EARTH

A strange story I heard
of Russians cut off by snow
without a priest to confess.
With their hands they dig the snow in compunction
and when finally emerges the face of the earth
they confide in tears and contrition
      the unendurable burden
speaking for hours and hours,
knowing perhaps
that the earth endures ...

Ashfield, Sydney
11.1.89

THE PSYCHE OF THE INANIMATE

The wallstones
the rooftiles
the windowpanes
or the floorslates
are not more alien to my body
than my nails, my hair
    my bones.

Ashfield, Sydney
13.1.89

32

EXPATRIATES

*For the deserted wife shall have more children
than she who lives with her husband.*
Galatians 4, 27

The artist outside his motherland
has chosen to be twice marginalised:
remote and ignored in his motherland
stranger and suspect in his adopted country.
But whoever experienced this double bereavement
exercises his soul in silence;
the Muses' nectar tastes differently
      when you taste it homeless
under the dominion of all four winds ...

Ashfield, Sydney
15.2.89

LYRICAL OBJECTION (B)

It is bigamy to love and to dream
Odysseus Elytis [5]

You can't love
without dreaming
nor dream
without loving.
Your embrace won't be complete,
        it won't be an embrace
if you don't open both arms.

Constantinople
24. 7. 89

TO MY MOTHER AGAIN

I admire that hill slope with the olive grove
that forty years ago and more you walked
every day carrying
>   the sudden orphanhood
>   the ultimate poverty
>   and a load like a beast of burden
to feed your many orphans.
It is impossible to collect the marks
of your naked, tortured foot
from the narrow roads of those bitter days
now washed out by wind and rain.
Yet your presence here is complete
refracted everywhere in the landscape
you possess my memory and my senses and
perhaps I taste unmediatedly as I swim
the water of your sweat and tears …

Ádele
2/3.8.89

THE MIRACLE

Miracle is not whatever transcends
your experience and imagination
the almost unexpected and therefore remote.
Miraculous is everything small or great
that you taste asleep or awake
every moment of the infinite day.

Carss Park, Sydney
7.10.89

RETURN TO THE SAME PLACE

Returning every year
to the same remote beach
you do not see the sand wrinkled
or the steep surface of rocks
brilliant armour of a speechless destiny.
So your return is never
a withdrawal or act of embarrassment;
by refolding only back on yourself
you can reconfirm the same oaths
you can count new losses.

Great Keppel Island
15.11.89

A PLACE IN UTOPIA

The only place
you can still breathe fresh air
is your absolute solitude
since even your friends
            rush to compromise.
There is nothing left for you now
but to explain to everyone
as persuasively as possible
the reason you can't follow them.

Athens
21.12.89

THE DRUNKARD

Staggering as he walks,
he is the most authentic dancer
        and initiator into human affairs.
He assures us that there forever exists
a drunkenness for anyone
and that the way goes on
even at an unstable pace.

Athens–Singapore
22.12.89

ONE DEFINITION MORE

Poetry means to risk at any moment
       your reliability
trying to reveal more tangibly
       the inexhaustible face
of things passing by.

Singapore–Melbourne
23.12.89

CAPTIVE

I was conquered at the edges of things
unable to escape for a single moment
the magic incessantly produced
in some neighbouring areas.

Carss Park, Sydney
31.12.89

MOST OF ALL

The ancient voice of earth
remains for me.
Leo Felipe [6]

If I was begging I wouldn't go
to humans only.
I admire the fidelity of dogs
cats' humbleness
swans' harmony.
Most of all
it's names I am begging for.

Carss Park, Sydney
22.2.90

THINGS AND MIRACLES

We have turned down the gift to
perceive things through our senses.
          Dimitris Mytarás [7]

No joy is complete
if it's not hailed by all senses.
Visions are deceitful phantoms
if you can't touch them
listen to their rhythmic breath
taste their blood and see
          that Christ is the Lord
be intoxicated by their sweat
at the noon of our brief life.

                    Ashfield, Sydney
                    27.2.90

43

BESIEGING THE INEFFABLE

A monk is a man apart from everyone
and united to everyone.
Evagrius Ponticus [8]

Poetry means taking possession of the world
not as your teachers and parents
have taught you
but as you dream of it
          in moments of wilderness:
in flashes of deliverance
          which signifies
the complete solidarity of creation.

Ashfield, Sydney
18.5.90

THE MUEZZIN

If it was for his voice
he would have won me a thousand times
but music does not suffice the soul
the miracle is accomplished even deeper
beyond logic, all senses beyond.

Constantinople
30.5.90

45

WHITENESS THE UNCONTENDED

When you dictate your thoughts to a scribe
you see the words run freely
unhesitant, undoubtful
questions silenced.
The white page that you face
          when you write yourself
is an impenetrable wall of light
a site of incarnate purity
pentelian marble immaculate.
So you are unable thus
to overcome the resistance of the white silence
so you see stains and shipwrecks
          in all letters.

Constantinople
2.6.90

DELIRIUM

Even when I broke a windowpane
      or a water glass
my Father and Mother always beat me
      for being careless.
But now, when by negligence I killed my sister
      why don't they beat me,
but kiss and hug me, why?

Singapore–Melbourne
18.7.90

NEVERTHELESS

... one hour from the real life of Odette, from the
real life of Odette when himself was not with her.
                                        Marcel Proust [9]

Despite our hypocrisy when we are not alone
our real life unfolds apocalyptically
only in coexistence with the other.
How can you talk without the other
and by saying who you are,
            know your own voice?
How can you measure sensitivity
which in muteness is hidden like shame
if you have no recognition of it in another?
You must admit that the other
is the only mirror which holds
            your complete figure.

                    Great Keppel Island
                    13.11.90

48

DAY AND NIGHT

Each day is a brief adventure
that you embark on, even gazing idly
        out the window;
sunlight then is your ally
it consoles you even if there is no
        water to drink
or dry bread on your table.
But needs are transformed into evil spirits
making your house uninhabitable
        and every hour unbearable
under the domination of night
which spreads shadows everywhere
and makes the slightest sound menacing;
the night is unaltered by light
symbol of the absolute blackness
        forever.

Ashfield, Sydney
5.1.91

49

FRUGALITY

All the villages we passed were so picturesque
on the way to Jervis Bay;
we felt a childish jealousy
for farmers and country workers
and the life we had not known
the pure pleasures and harvesting of earth.
Unable to move there
we brought with us to the city
at least the music of their names:
Kiama, Nowra, Berry, Vincentia.

Redfern, Sydney
9.1.91

50

NOTHING IN EXCESS

Poetry neither boasts
      nor laments.
The measure does not abide in extremities;
it walks unpretentiously like a dove
in the perennial documents of your language.
And if someday you are moved to follow
the word down to the start of its root
you will find yourself face to face with the dove.

Gosford
19.1.91

PRESENCE

Looking into your eyes
for the first time I realised
how deep this flat world
      can be.
Touching your hand I believed
that despite my all-encompassing solitude
I hold unfathomable reserves
      to tame the Abyss.
Listening silent to your voice
I felt all self-preserving resistance
melt like a candle of the Resurrection
I felt the arguments of reason
      refuted without reasoning.

Ashfield, Sydney
22.1.91

MEMORIES

They have nothing to do
with the flow of time;
they are clefts
through which crept into the soul
        light of another world
and the soul was immersed in its own full moon
proud there to meet the coming night.

Ashfield, Sydney
11.3.91

53

TRIAL

Children run in the streets as if in
revenge for the stillness of the dead.
Tàsos Leivaditis[10]

In our most private gestures
mostly we hide ourselves from children;
not because we'll be seen and exposed,
but because they start asking
those perpetual questions
        of innocent wonder.
Implacable they are, all children's questions
not just because they query indiscriminately
but because they transform the obvious to a riddle
and see the miraculous all around.

Ashfield, Sydney
16.3.91

THE GREAT DILEMMA

No one knows when he is more useful
to himself and others:
when he struggles and drives them elsewhere,
      expanding the horizon by resistance,
or when he departs in dignity
leaving all space incontestable
      to the responsibility of others.

Ashfield, Sydney
16.3.91

THE TIMELESS MIRACLE

Childhood has no age;
it is grace bestowed only on those
who resign from their age
        and their generation
searching tirelessly
for the timeless miracle in every face;
aware that humans are the Light.

Ashfield, Sydney
16.3.91

INTEGRITY

Whoever expresses himself in gestures only
    appears fragmented
    a mutilated flute.
Our body however rests in plenitude
speaking with all its limbs
    and all scents
    all colours all secretions;
and especially with inarticulate fears
epitomised in shame.

Ashfield, Sydney
5.4.91

THE POET'S RACE

They have a strange ability
to tell you simple things
and embarrass you that until now
these passed your eyes unnoticed.
Every embroidery depends
on single fine stitches—
humbleness and patience which force
a blind surface to bloom
            in immaculate jasmines.
Great truths are neglected
            in absolute transparency
since people picture them
            on unapproachable heights:
the original sin of thinkers
            who imagine themselves outstanding.

Ashfield, Sydney
6.4.91

A GRIEF COLLECTIVE AND MULTIFARIOUS

Every limb of Your divine flesh...
Matins of Good Friday

A sealed house is not simply
a unit out of use,
            an impenetrable bulk of silence
which marks absence in one word.
It is a grief collective and multifarious
whether its landlord died long ago
or is still on distant travels.
Doors present another dolour
            being closed
nailed shutters another complaint
            unshaken by the wind.
Walls freeze without breath and voice;
utensils in closets and drawers
            are paralysed
all furniture longs for the duster,
mirrors have swallowed all forms
and stayed immobilised
            like boas in hibernation.
Everything in a sealed house proclaims
            a time of death,
procedures of perdition.
Yet every limb preserves
even in decomposition
its own distinct invocation.

Ashfield, Sydney
9.4.91

59

ABOVE ALL ELSE CHARITABLE

Obscurity innately twitches
Kikí Dimoulá [11]

If you speak literally your words will be
    of one direction
few people will be consoled
    and that is not your intention.
By hinting you open horizons
    to all probabilities of infinity,
you smoothe the sharp ends of immediacy
avoiding redundant injuries;
only then is your word apt and vivid
    and above all else, charitable.

Ashfield, Sydney
20.4.91

BITTER EQUATION

Each one carries his own problem;
and though he thinks day by day
       to pace closer to its solution,
gradually that problem marks his life
and becomes his very physiognomy.
So when we happen to meet someone,
instead of suggesting another version,
       a new person,
we reveal yet another deadlock,
       our problem.

Sydney–Melbourne
27.4.91

FROM A DISTANCE

Whenever I go to the window
I see him walking aimlessly
in his small garden,
a drab backyard with the rotary clothesline
          and the rabbits,
          my Polish neighbour.

We never had the chance to talk
          and I haven't heard his voice;
I never dared to wave
since I have no answers to his puzzles
which I guess almost infallibly—
          from a distance.

Sydney–Melbourne
27.4.91

SILENT ALLEGORY

And the candle flames at nights shaken by the wind of
some primordial forgiveness—whom does it forgive?
                                    Tàsos Leivaditis[10]

Tonight all scenes of dusk
have something of the uncertainty,
the sacred infinitude I mean
often found in the brushstrokes
            of a modern painter.
Geometric shapes and balanced lines
            are unable to encapsulate
all that silent allegory
            called present life.
We are still beginners
            in deciphering the world
despite children and drunkards
            who teach us
everlastingly and without any arrogance
the elements of the authentic alphabet.

                            Ashfield, Sydney
                            14.7.91

63

THE AFFIRMATIVE GLANCE

Poetry, the affirmative glance
         of God
through the mortal eyes
         of humans.
It evaluates the deeds of the Seven Days
which in the beginning had no "blemish
or wrinkle or any such thing"
and grants them anew the remission
to end as they began:
         very good indeed.

Ashfield, Sydney
1.11.91

BORROWED PATERNITY

These lines I hastily record
        are not mine;
otherwise I could write
        at any moment—
and certainly that is always my desire.
Well, some indeterminate voice
        whispers verses in the air,
but to catch them I must be alone
        and strangest of all
I must be deeply hurt
        by the events
        and, above all, by all human
        beings.

Great Keppel Island
14.11.91

ON THE TRAIL

Some day we should become mature enough
to judge humans not as the sum
of their deeds and words,
but from their tone of voice
         an absent-minded glance
         a clumsy gesture.
In such isolated fragments
incomplete but authentic
an icon of our neighbour lies hidden;
not in the futile attempt
to harmonise for social assessment
elements dissimilar by nature.

Ashfield, Sydney
8.12.91

THE OTHER LEVEL

All become the same when
taken by perdition.
Kikí Dimoulá [11]

It is the solidarity of disaster
the fear of the irrevocable absence
that familiarises vanished things
    to one another.
It is the airy nature
    also of memories
that avoids sharp endings,
and the silent forgiveness
    of nostalgia
for faces and things and situations
that performs that alchemy
which holds life up
    to another level.

Ashfield, Sydney
16.12.91

67

THE AUTHENTICITY OF SIGNATURE

And yet, the question is not
how we talk;
the supreme lesson left for us
is the style of silence
that will seal with its signature
any memorable gesture.

Ashfield, Sydney
16.5.87

NOTES

1. Gregory Nazianzus, fourth-century Father of the Church.

2. Dimitris Maronitis, contemporary Neohellenist.

3. C. P. Cavafy, modern Greek poet (1863–1933).

4. Protagoras, famous Sophist of the fifth century BC.

5. Odysseus Elytis, modern Greek poet (Nobel Prize 1979) (1911–   ).

6. Leo Felipe, modern Spanish poet.

7. Dimitris Mytarás, modern Greek painter.

8. Evagrius Ponticus, sixth-century monk & mystic of the Greek Orthodox Church.

9. Marcel Proust, modern French prose writer (1871–1922).

10. Tàsos Leivaditis, contemporary Greek poet (1921–1988).

11. Kikí Dimoulá, contemporary Greek poet.

CONTENTS

About the Author

Stylianos S. Charkianakis was born in Rethymnon, Crete in 1935. He studied at the Orthodox Theological School of Chalki, Constantinople. He was awarded a Doctorate in Divinity from the University of Athens. He studied later at the University of Bonn, Germany, where he earned a post-graduate degree in theology. For eight years he was Associate Professor of Systematic Theology at the University of Thesallonika, Greece. In 1970 he was ordained as titular Metropolitan of Miletoupolis. He become the Abbot of the Historical Monastery of Vlatades at Thesallonika, and one of the founding members of the Institute of Patristic Studies and the chairman of the board of directors. He came to Australia in 1975 where he took up his position as Primate of the Greek Orthodox Church. Seventeen volumes of his poetry have been published in Athens. He was been awarded two prizes: the International Gottfried von Herder Prize Vienna 1973 for his contribution to the ecumenical movement and culture in general, and the Academy of Athens Prize for Poetry 1980. He lives in Sydney.

About the Translator

V. Karalis was born in 1960. He teaches Modern Greek at the University of Sydney.

COLOPHON

These poems are set in the typeface
Goudy Modern, designed by the American Frederic W.
Goudy (1865–1947). He was much inspired by the British craftsman
William Morris, and became one of the finest and most prolific type
designers in history. Goudy designed over 100 types and displayed some of
his finest in his periodical *Ars Typographica*. In 1939 seventy-five of his
designs were destroyed by fire. Goudy always wanted his work to be not
only at the service of the limited edition and the private patron, but also to
serve the general printer in town and country. Goudy Modern reads easily
with its weight so nicely judged and the thicks and thins so cleverly adjusted
to give a generous and open effect. The thin lines are cunningly relieved
with perfectly-calculated thins, giving what is almost a bold face a very
pleasantly light effect when leaded, in this case by Shirley Williams at
Primavera Press. The paper is *Terra Firma* 110 gsm all-cotton paper with
laid-lines made by Australian Paper. This paper meets with requirements
of AS 4003 (Int), *Permanent Uncoated Paper and Paperboard*. The cover
is *Banksia Felt* 260 gsm, acid-free and archival. This book was issued
in a softcover edition of 1000 copies. Besides the trade edition,
a limited edition was issued with *Coptic Binding* by bookbinders
David Newbold and Terry Collins. The timber boards of
Norfolk Island Pine, supplied by Joe Christian,were fashioned
by Bob Howard and carved by laser. The limited edition is
numbered 1–100, with numbers 10 –100 offered for sale.

P.B.

74